Nocturnal Animals
Tarsiers

Kristin Petrie
ABDO Publishing Company

visit us at
www.abdopublishing.com

Published by ABDO Publishing Company, 8000 West 78th Street, Edina, Minnesota 55439.
Copyright © 2010 by Abdo Consulting Group, Inc. International copyrights reserved in all
countries. No part of this book may be reproduced in any form without written permission from the
publisher. The Checkerboard Library™ is a trademark and logo of ABDO Publishing Company.

Printed in the United States of America, North Mankato, Minnesota.
082009
012010

 PRINTED ON RECYCLED PAPER

Cover Photo: Alamy
Interior Photos: Alamy pp. 6, 8, 19; Getty Images pp. 1, 13, 16; iStockphoto pp. 5, 15;
    Peter Arnold p. 7; Photolibrary pp. 10, 17; Sandlin Associates Stock Footage Library p. 21

Series Coordinator: Megan M. Gunderson
Editors: Heidi M.D. Elston, Megan M. Gunderson
Art Direction & Cover Design: Neil Klinepier

Library of Congress Cataloging-in-Publication Data

Petrie, Kristin, 1970-
  Tarsiers / Kristin Petrie.
     p. cm. -- (Nocturnal animals)
  Includes index.
  ISBN 978-1-60453-739-0
  1. Tarsiers--Juvenile literature. I. Title.
  QL737.P965P48 2010
  599.8'3--dc22
                 2009025657

Contents

Tarsiers. 4

Tiny Jumpers. 6

Tropical Homes. 8

Nighttime Senses. 10

True Carnivores 12

Young Tarsiers 14

Natural Enemies. 16

Human Threats. 18

At Risk 20

Glossary 22

Web Sites. 23

Index. 24

Tarsiers

What animal looks like a monkey and jumps like a frog? It can even turn its head like an owl! This creature has a long tail and lengthy fingers and toes. Its teeth are sharp, and it chows down only on live animals.

The first things you will notice about this creature are its eyes. They are huge! In fact, its eyes are bigger than its brain. This tiny, little-known creature is called the tarsier.

Tarsiers are closely related to **primates** such as humans and monkeys. They are nocturnal mammals that belong to the order Primates. Within their order, tarsiers make up the family **Tarsiidae**. And, they are the only members of the genus *Tarsius*.

Nocturnal, Diurnal, or Crepuscular?

One way scientists group animals is by when they are most active. Nocturnal animals work and play during the night and sleep during the day. Diurnal animals are the opposite. They rest at night and are active during the day. Crepuscular animals are most active at twilight. This includes the time just before sunrise or just after sunset.

There are at least eight tarsier species. And, scientists continue to discover new ones. Each tarsier species differs in small ways. They may have larger eyes, longer feet, or hairier tails. Their **habitats** or favorite foods may be different. Keep reading! There is much to discover about these wide-eyed little critters.

Scientists use a method called scientific classification to sort organisms into groups. The basic classification system includes eight groups. In descending order, they are domain, kingdom, phylum, class, order, family, genus, and species.

Tiny Jumpers

The tarsier is one strange-looking creature! It must be huge, right? Wrong! The average tarsier weighs just 3 to 6 ounces (80 to 165 g). Its head and body measure only 3.5 to 6 inches (9 to 16 cm) tall. Its long tail adds another 5 to 11 inches (13.5 to 27.5 cm). Can you believe all those features fit on such a tiny animal?

Short, thick, silky fur covers the tarsier's small body. Its backside can be gray to dark brown. The underside may be lighter.

The tarsier's second and third toes have claws for grooming. The rest of its fingers and toes end in nails.

*Leaping tarsiers move
extremely quietly.*

The tarsier's enormous eyes are locked in place on its round head. Luckily, the tarsier has a special way to view its surroundings. It can turn its head 180 degrees in each direction!

The head also has two twitchy, bald ears. They constantly swivel, crinkle up, and unfold. This helps the tarsier listen for predators and prey.

The tarsier's fingers and toes end in soft, flat pads. These help the tarsier cling to almost any surface. The long tail also supports the tarsier in its perch.

Extra long tarsals, or anklebones, give the tarsier its name. The tarsier's long legs make up one-quarter of its weight. These large, muscular limbs are made for serious leaping. The tarsier can jump an astounding 16 to 20 feet (5 to 6 m)!

Tropical Homes

Tarsiers are native to several Southeast Asian island nations. These include Brunei, Indonesia, Malaysia, and the Philippines. Different species are native to certain islands within these countries. Some are even named for their home island. You can probably guess where the Sangihe Island tarsier is found!

Many types of forests support these **arboreal** creatures. Tarsiers will even live in secondary forests. These younger forests appear after original forests have been destroyed. Tarsiers will also live among plantation crops, including coconuts and nutmeg.

Tarsiers are usually found less than three to seven feet (1 to 2 m) above the ground. When sleeping, some will hang out higher up. Tarsiers snooze in tangles of vegetation or sometimes in hollow trees. Some species have one favorite sleeping site, while others use three or four.

If bothered, tarsiers will change sleeping sites.

DETAIL RANGE MAP

Philippines

Brunei

Malaysia

Indonesia

Where Tarsiers Live

Nighttime Senses

Since the tarsier is nocturnal, it spends daytime hours fast asleep. When sunset comes, it gets moving! The tarsier hunts, travels, rests, and socializes at night.

The tarsier's sense organs are specially adapted for its nocturnal lifestyle. First, its huge eyes allow in lots of light. Some nocturnal animals also have a tapetum, which helps their eyes work well at night. Tarsiers have a fovea instead. This special structure is packed with cells that give the tarsier sharper vision.

Besides sight, the tarsier relies on its excellent senses of smell and hearing for survival. All three senses are a must for hunting and communicating in the dark!

A tarsier will mark its own territory with scents. Getting a whiff of a stranger's smell may tell a tarsier, "Get lost! Private property!" All night long, the tarsier listens for predators and prey. And, it makes and hears many different tarsier calls. These may include distress calls and even nightly songs with a mate.

Why is the tapetum missing? Some scientists believe the tarsier's ancestors were diurnal and did not rely on night vision.

Nocturnal Eyes

Some lucky nocturnal animals have special eye features that help them in the dark. They may have large eyes compared to their body size. Also, their pupils may open wider than ours do in low light. These two features allow more light to enter their eyes.

After light enters an eye's pupil, the lens focuses it on the retina. In the retina, two special kinds of cells receive the light. These are rods and cones.

Rods work in low light. They detect size, shape, and brightness. Cones work in bright light. They detect color and details. Nocturnal animals often have many more rods than cones.

Many nocturnal eyes also have a tapetum lucidum behind the retina. The tapetum is like a mirror. Light bounces off of it and back through the retina a second time. This gives the light another chance to strike the rods. The reflected light then continues back out through the pupil. This causes the glowing eyes you may see at night!

NIGHT ANIMAL

DAY ANIMAL

RETINA

RETINA

RODS

CONES

TAPETUM LUCIDUM

RETINA

LENS

PUPIL

ANIMAL'S EYE (side view)

True Carnivores

For such a tiny creature, the tarsier is fierce at mealtime. For one thing, the tarsier eats only live animals. If you offered a tarsier a delicious dead beetle, it would just hop away. But what if the tarsier saw that same beetle alive and skittering by? It would pounce and kill!

A tarsier's diet depends on its species and the season. Yet no matter its species, insects are the tarsier's favorite food. Tarsiers eat grasshoppers, butterflies, cicadas, ants, and other bugs. Some also prey on snakes, birds, bats, and other small animals. They may even eat frogs and freshwater crabs!

It is interesting to watch a tarsier catch its prey. It begins by listening for the faint sounds of bugs and small animals. Next, it turns its owl-like neck and locks its eyes on the prey. The tarsier then pounces and grabs the critter with both hands. Some tarsiers even grab prey right out of the air! The tarsier kills its victim with its sharp teeth. Often, it returns to its perch to eat.

The tarsier has been called the world's most carnivorous primate.

Young Tarsiers

A tarsier's life starts with the mating of a male and a female. Depending on her species, the female gives birth five to six months after mating. She has just one baby tarsier at a time.

At birth, a tarsier weighs around .8 ounces (23 g). That may sound tiny. Yet this is nearly one-third of its adult weight. That would be like a 150-pound (70-kg) human giving birth to a 50-pound (20-kg) baby!

The newborn tarsier is born with fur and open eyes. It can climb and leap soon after birth. A **captive** tarsier will begin hunting its own food around 37 days. A wild tarsier may begin earlier. Yet, it may not successfully catch prey until it is 45 days old. Depending on her species, the mother stops nursing her baby after about 80 days.

How long does the tarsier live? In captivity, one tarsier lived to be 16 years old. In the wild, that great question has not yet been answered. Scientists still have much to learn about this charming creature.

A mother tarsier often parks her infant on a branch while she searches for food. Young tarsiers are too heavy to carry around all the time!

Natural Enemies

Excellent hearing helps tarsiers avoid predators.

Tarsiers are **aggressive** predators. With their great senses and amazing jumps, they are feared by their prey! So, what predators do tarsiers fear?

These lucky little creatures have few natural enemies to worry about. Owls and civets are two of their main natural predators. Like tarsiers, these animals are nocturnal. So, they are up and watchful when tarsiers are awake and leaping. Tarsiers must also watch out for monitor lizards. Even **domestic** dogs and cats may attack tarsiers.

Tree-dwelling snakes present another threat. But, spectral tarsiers will actually work as a group against a threatening snake. They will lunge and make threatening noises at it. Some tarsiers may even bite the snake!

On average, spectral tarsiers live in groups of three. However, members of other groups will join in fighting a predator.

Human Threats

Humans are the tarsier's number one enemy. People take tarsiers from the wild to sell as pets. On some islands, they hunt these little creatures for food. And, **pesticides** used to protect crops sometimes poison tarsiers by mistake.

The greatest harm comes from human destruction of the tarsier's **habitat**. People remove trees for logging and to make room for plantations. This deforestation is to a tarsier what bulldozing your house would be to you! Where would you sleep? What would you eat?

Deforestation can lead to extinction. Animals lose their homes and are pushed into smaller territories. Sometimes, tarsiers can survive even if deforestation changes their habitats. However, their preferred sleeping sites must remain. Otherwise, the species may be in trouble.

Humans may be the tarsier's main enemy. However, many people are working hard to protect these fascinating creatures and their habitats.

At Risk

It is difficult to determine the tarsier's **status**. Their nocturnal habits and small populations make them difficult to study. Still, several species are known to be **endangered**. Deforestation, **pesticides**, forest fires, and hunting all threaten their survival.

Education is needed to help protect the tarsier. Some farmers mistakenly believe tarsiers are eating their crops. So, they kill them. What many farmers don't realize is that tarsiers can actually be helpful. Because of their diet, tarsiers may help farmers get rid of real pests such as grasshoppers!

Hunting particularly threatens the Siau Island tarsier. On Siau Island, they are eaten five to ten at a time as a snack called *tola-tola*. Today, there are only a few thousand Siau Island tarsiers remaining. In fact, this tarsier species is one of the World's 25 Most Endangered **Primates**.

Preserving their **habitats** is the only way to maintain tarsier populations. This is because tarsiers rarely survive for long in **captivity**. Scientists struggle to breed them in zoos and labs. Therefore, the tarsier and its habitat must be respected and protected!

Protecting forests will help save the Siau Island tarsier and its relatives.

Glossary

aggressive (uh-GREH-sihv) - displaying hostility.

arboreal (ahr-BAWR-ee-uhl) - living in or frequenting trees.

captive - captured and held against one's will. Captivity is the state of being captive.

domestic - tame, especially relating to animals.

endangered - in danger of becoming extinct.

habitat - a place where a living thing is naturally found.

pesticide (PEHS-tuh-side) - a substance used to kill pests.

primate - any mammal belonging to the order Primates. Primates share features such as grasping hands or feet. Humans, monkeys, apes, and lemurs are primates.

status - a state or a condition.

Tarsiidae (tahr-SEYE-uh-dee) - the scientific name for the tarsier family.

Web Sites

To learn more about tarsiers, visit ABDO Publishing Company on the World Wide Web at **www.abdopublishing.com**. Web sites about tarsiers are featured on our Book Links page. These links are routinely monitored and updated to provide the most current information available.

Index

B
body 6
Brunei 8

C
captivity 14, 20
classification 4, 5
coat 5, 6, 14
color 6
communication 10, 17
conservation 20

D
defense 7, 10, 17
deforestation 8, 18, 20
diet 4, 5, 7, 10, 12, 14, 16, 20

E
ears 7
enemies 7, 10, 16, 17, 18, 20
eyes 4, 5, 7, 10, 12, 14

F
feet 5
fingers 4, 7

H
habitat 5, 8, 18, 20
hands 12
head 4, 6, 7
hunting 7, 10, 12, 14, 16

I
Indonesia 8

J
jumping 4, 7, 12, 14, 16, 17

L
legs 7
life cycle 14
life span 14

M
Malaysia 8

P
pads 7
pets 18
Philippines 8
primates 4, 20
Primates (order) 4

R
reproduction 14

S
scent marking 10
senses 7, 10, 12, 16
size 4, 5, 6, 7, 12, 14
sleeping 8, 10, 18
socializing 10

T
tail 4, 5, 6, 7
Tarsiidae (family) 4
Tarsius (genus) 4
teeth 4, 12
territory 10, 18
toes 4, 7

Y
young 14